Bristol Radical Pamphlet

Radical Brewing

Work, Energy, Commoning & Beer

Steve Stuffit

ISBN 978-1-911522-11-9

Bristol Radical History Group. 2009.
www.brh.org.uk ~ brh@brh.org.uk

Part 1 – A Microhistory of Brewing

The ancient process of making a fermented drink, whilst a simple chemical reaction between yeast and starches, contains many more parallels to contemporary life than might at first be apparent. This short microhistory considers the struggles for land, degradation of ecologies, revolutionary means of production, vast increase in the breadth and depth of markets, attacks on time, mono-crop agriculture versus wildcraft and how the transition from herb to hop helped facilitate a logistic revolution.

Pre-Enclosures, The Church and the Herbs

Ale is thousands of years old. Its use in the UK can be seen from the 6th Century onwards, when accessing wild honey, the main component of mead, became something of an elite practice. Ale contains malt grain (usually barley), water and yeast. Herbs can be added to this mix, both for flavour and for their preservative qualities. What was added depended on the local ecology, examples in medieval times include yarrow, wormwood, mugwort, sage, heather, oak bark, dandelion roots or leaves, juniper berries and branches, nettles, and ground ivy (also known as alehoof).

Some of these herbs had psychoactive and narcotic properties. They were uppers rather than sedatives like hops, which were the main ingredient in ale's successor beer. Ale could be viewed as a drink appropriate to the pre-Christian pagan culture with the myriad of festivals and rites connected to the rhythm and 'use value' of the land, rather than the industrialised rhythm of waged labour associated with beer. The incoming Church christianised festivals and adopted indigenous rites and customs in order to get some sort of leverage with commoners. This process of assimilation also led them into the brewing game.

Most history books record how the Church quickly became involved in the trade by establishing the monopoly on a certain mix of herbs called 'Gruit'. The main components of this mix were sweet gale (*Myrica gale*), yarrow (*Achillea millefolium*) and marsh rosemary (*Ledum palustre*) supplemented with various other additions. These herbs were grown in monastery gardens, though access would have been widely available in the surrounding ecologies. It is unclear how or even if it was possible for the Church to enforce a Gruit monopoly if access to these herbs was so widespread.

Alewives and the Alehouse

Pre-10th Century brewing was mostly a decentralised and transitory process. Brewing and selling took place in domestic households normally by women called 'alewives'.

The History of Beer and Brewing explains how widespread brewing was, and how what we can think of as the first pubs developed: "Gradually alewives or brewsters became so celebrated in their communities that people would go into their houses to drink and eventually buy ale." When a brew was ready the ale wife would put a long pole called an 'ale-stake' outside the house – transforming the home into a public space, into an 'alehouse'.

The alehouse was a cross-class opportunity for women to increase their income. As well as the wives of wealthier men who brewed for domestic needs selling off the surplus, there was a mobile class of itinerant poor many of whom would set up an alehouse in a village before moving on.

Control of the Alehouse, Subverting The Church and State

In the 10th Century the puritanical King Edgar ordered the closing of many alehouses and allowed only one per village. He also ordered that none drink "..more than a peg", a reference to an attempt to control the amount of drink taken in one draught by the placing of pegs inside drinking vessels. This vessel then became the basis of competitive drinking games and the expression 'taking someone down a peg or two'. Commoners not only revolted against measurement but they also subverted some of the Church's celebrations. Dunstan (who advised Edgar) issued Canon No. 28 saying: "Let men be very temperate at church wakes and pray earnestly and suffer there no drinking or unseemliness." 'Church wakes' were organised on the evening before a saint's day, and people were expected to kneel and sit in prayer to 'wake' during the night. Apparently this became boring:

> The pepul fell to lecherie, and song and daunces, with harping and piping, and also to glotony and sinne; and so turned the holiness to cursydness.

Eventually church wakes were replaced by fairs held on or near the saint's days.

Until the 13th Century there were periods when the alewives were forbidden from brewing, one of them being the occasions when the church was holding a 'church ale'. This was a compulsory festival where locals would contribute ales to a collective pot from which they would then have to buy, the funds going back to the church. Commoners resisted this. In areas covered by forest, outside the jurisdiction of any authorities, villagers would gather together and donate their 'scots' or shares to their own common pot and party for days. They were getting off 'scot free'. The Church and State responded with attempts to ban these occasions with the Bishop of Durham stating, "...moreover we forbid scot-ales and games in sacred places".

Of particular interest are 'bede-ales'. These were drinking parties arranged to raise money because "an honest man decayed in his fortune is set up again by the liberal benevolence and contribution of friends at a feast". Then there were 'bride-ales', a wedding day contribution by the parents of the bride, which friends would contribute what they liked in payment for it. In 1468 the Prior of Canterbury ordained that, "potations made in churches commonly called give-ales or bride-ales should be discontinued under penalty of excommunication". By the end of the century the first licensing statue under Henry VII was issued, empowering the authorities "to reject and put away common ale selling in towns and places where they should think convenient and to take sureties of keepers of ale-houses in their good behaving". This, in effect, banned informal 'benefit gigs', leading to a more centralised control of the brewing trade.

Tithes, Wages and Taxes

Until the end of the 12th Century there were no special taxes on brewing, although it was still used to extract value from workers for private profit. Ale was regarded as an item of food and as such figured in the food 'rents' or 'tithes' payable to the Crown, Church or local lord. Between 690 and 693 King Ine of Wessex issued a law, No.70 section 1, which refers to a list of payments in kind in return for land. Ale is included in the list and suggests that families who have land do in fact brew, showing how widespread domestic brewing was.

In addition to the alewives, the monastic and manorial landlords were the main brewers and up until the 13th Century paid up to two thirds of laboures' wages in ale. This practice was challenged by the Peasants Revolt, which won actual wage increases rather than payment in kind. By the 14th Century there was a corresponding increase in the number of alehouses, presumably to spend some of the cash wage on ale.

The first national tax levied under Henry II in 1188 funded the crusades. This war tax entitled the state to the value of 1/10 of all 'movables' (including ale) in the Kingdom, and was known as the 'Saladin tithe'. Article 35 of the Magna Carta decreed a standard measure for 'wine, ale and corn'. Standardisation, aside from its portrayed benefits of establishing 'good methods', was also a way of spreading the rule of law and limiting varieties or consolidating practices - in short to expand trade, especially in malt. Once a standard had been established it usually spread to areas whose customs may be entirely different.

Regulation and Profit

In 1266 Henry III established the 'Assize of Bread and Ale', relating the price of bread and ale to the cost of wheat and malt. This established a country wide price index that was portrayed as keeping ale affordable. To enforce these regulations the local authorities appointed 'ale conners' whose job it would be to inspect ales. The custom of displaying an ale-stake when a brew was ready became more significant as it became an offence to offer for sale of a brew without an ale-stake. It was also an offence to offer more than one brew under the same stake. The stake was now the signal to the ale-conner to perform his duty.

Fines extracted for contravening these regulations became the Crown's way of extracting profit from the brewing activities of others, in the same way that the Church did with church ales. It seems to have become a de facto licensing system for the Lord of the Manor, as those breaking the assize (i.e the majority) were brought before a court and fined. For many, this court appearance became an annual event.

Additionally the assize, by fixing the price of ale to the price of grains, invited the brewer to reduce the strength of his ale, thus obtaining greater gallonage to the quarter of malt and "incidentally increasing his income" (a practice which continues today).

Refusal of Work

In 1544 there appears to have been a struggle over time, and the conditions of work. It was reported that there was an excessive number of alehouses in the city of Coventry and that many inhabitants had left their accustomed trades to become brewers and tipplers, "whereby Almightie God is highlie displeased, the comenwealthe of this City greatly decayed". The Coventry Leet book (a form of court records) records it was ordered that no labourers were to use inns or alehouses on working days:

> And forasmuch as it is daylye seen that they whiche be of the pooreste sorte doo sytee all day in the ale-house drynkynge and playnge at the Cardes and tables and spend all that they can get prodigally upon themselves to the highe displeasure of God .

Large scale brewing was previously dominated by the monasteries but developing alongside them were commercial common breweries. They were competing capitals, but in the transition from feudalism into market based capitalism, large landowners took over the monasteries and the stage was set for the appearance of the hop.

Enclosures and Beyond

> Now dig it and leave it, for sun for to burn, and afterwards fence it, to serve for that turn.
>
> *The hop for his profit I thus do exalt*, it strenghteneth drink, and it favoureth malt.
>
> Thomas Tusser, *Five Hundred Points of Good Husbandry*, 16th Century

The hop, a relative of the wild stinging nettle, revolutionised the means and methods of production, destroying old markets and enabling a technologically-driven expansion. The arrival of the hop appears to be preceded by woolen capitalism. Wool left England from Norwich and Ipswich to be finished in Flanders. Flemish weavers were encouraged to migrate to England and finish the cloth here before exporting it, and with them they brought a cargo of beer.

Beer is different from ale in that it uses a different brewing technique and uses hops as a flavourer and preservative. The vast variety of ales were now able to be produced from local ingredients available to all, starting to become reduced into a simpler product.

Changing Land, Gender, Energy

The hop couldn't have developed in this way without the process of enclosure

Organised around the profitability of wool and sheep these massive land evictions led to the creation of a new class of landless commoners restricted from accessing their needs from the commons. The shift to the greater use of hops was described by historian Peter Mathias in The Brewing Industry in England as a "slow change in public taste encouraged by brewers searching for greater efficiency in their product."

There is nothing 'natural' here about hop use. It was the economic expression of a ruling class that permanently modified how local ecologies were viewed and used. The argument that hops brought greater 'efficiency' to beer due to its preservative properties is undermined by the fact that herbs used in ale production like yarrow, bog myrtle and rosemary also have preservative qualities. In many 'history of beer-type' books the use of herbs is attributed solely to 'flavour', overlooking what were sophisticated examples of peasant technology and folk wisdom.

The main regions of hop growing were located in Kent due to the advanced enclosures and the capital available to the rich yeoman farmers to invest in the initial systems of production necessary to get a high yield. Between 1500-1640 hopped beer superseded ale and brewing, which had traditionally been done in villages by alewives, became a (male) urban occupation. As a consequence of the amounts of capital needed to retool to hop production, breweries tended to become larger and more concentrated business enterprises.

As Steven Easrnshaw notes in *The Pub in Literature:*

> ..a change in the role played by earlier alewives in the subsistence survival of their family or their own widowhood, to the industrial capitalist ideas of thrift and disciplined work that were beginning to emerge in the 17C,. Thus they are alewives and brewsters as long as there is no serious profit to be made. When brewing becomes economically viable on a larger scale women are ousted. They become barmaids and landlord's appendages

The 16th Century poem The Tunning of Elynour Rummyng, by the priest John Skelton, talks of the alewife and witch as related to "..the devil and she be sib". Also, in Witchcraft In Early Modern Europe the authors describe the effect of this propaganda in creating popular representations undermining the position of the alewife by questioning their morals, ability to brew and general trustworthiness – in doing so opening the doors to the male brewers.

As well as requiring a change in land use facilitated by the enclosures, hops required a change in energy use. The process of making beer with hops is more fuel intensive due to the necessity for longer and higher temperatures. This led to the substitution of wood for coal, which further concentrated production in the hands of those with access to capital, and alienated rural production, especially since gleaning (using rights to access fire wood) was now prohibited.

Beer brewed with hops kept longer than ale, meaning that the distribution radius widened, leading to a deepening and broadening of markets. By the 16th Century brewing was the largest industry in England. Along the banks of the Thames large breweries starting sinking their own wells. This needed large amounts of private capital, leading to a concentration of the industry. By the end of the 18th Century Meux, a brewer in London installed 24 huge vats, one of which contained 1,296,000 pints. The beer brewed in this area was called 'porter' (being popular with London's market porters) and could be brewed and stored in bulk, moving production from the home into the factory. It used cheaper ingredients than other beers and the brewing process meant that more could be extracted from the malt needing less hops. It could be brewed for more months of the year and huge profits were made.

The huge debt-based growth and speculative capital of the past thirty years is really nothing new. Hops was a speculators' crop that attracted a vast army of middlemen who profited solely from the capital they invested outside of any productive 'value'. The amount of capital and labour needed for hop production then "..clearly limited its appeal for the small holder or subsistence farmer." - Rogers, History of Agriculture and Prices in England VI.

As well as the speculation on the plant, in the late 1880s breweries were floated on the stock exchange "..having the effect of making the erstwhile private proprietor extremely rich and influential men with financial resources they were able to invest outside the brewing industry ...". This in itself led to a situation where brewers had to grow, as the Country Brewer's Gazette put it in 1897: "As leases fall brewers are obliged to find further outlets for their beer..there is so much capital on which to pay interest"

'Pale ale' came about through a change in fuel use. Coke fired kilns resulted in paler malt than that produced by burning wood. It kept for longer, enabling export of large quantities of beer to overseas colonial markets like India. This expansion abroad coincided with the temperance movement that was impinging on the growth of the domestic market. Sugar was transformed during the second half of the 18th Century from an upper class luxury to a working class 'necessity'. Between 1700 and 1800 British per capita consumption of sugar rose by almost 500%. Sugar was an essential part of the industrial diet. It was a cheap source of calories that give the body a quick energy boost, saving on time and fuel for food preparation. Sugar had been mainly used in tea, but also became part of beer production. The extra value extracted from overseas colonial slave labour was directly transferred into beer as the cheap slave-produced sugar was substituted for the more expensive malts.

The evolution of the brewing industry from 1900 until the current day is basically more of the same. We can see a repetition of patterns and processes over time, always justified (in hindsight) as 'neutral' changes in 'public taste' or 'efficiency'. Now there is a greater concentration of the means of production than ever before. As Linda Hill, co-author of *Alcohol, No Ordinary Commodity*, says:

> Consolidation after mergers = savings = 'investment in brands'. There are no huge secrets in making lager or ethanol, so the key to profitability in the alcohol industry is marketing linked to image, lifestyle and emotions. I think the way we sometimes think about the industry – as the historic little local brewery or whisky-maker, and our favourite pub – can be pretty out of date. With a globalised industry, economies of scale and profitability make marketing and policy influence a whole new ball game.

Pubs themselves have become a commodity subject to the makeover whims of unaccountable managers (think of theme pubs), whilst tenants become more and more separated from their livelihoods, much like the commoners were from their production. See *Last Orders for the Local - Working Class Space – v - the Market Place: Theme Pubs and Other Environmental Disasters* from the *Revolt Against Plenty* website for a highly inspiring contemporary history of beer, with prospects for resistance.

The Future

This year there are large scale hop shortages predicted across both EU and USA. They aren't caused by an ecological 'scarcity' per se (although climate change for one is playing a part with droughts and floods and fires) but the result of a conversion of previously hop-farmed land into ethanol-producing crops for fuel.

Because of this it is possible that breweries will adulterate their product, reduce the strength and raise the price to pass on the extra cost to drinkers rather than let their profits take the hit. With home brew far easier to make than many technocrats would have you believe, and with ingredients working out at 40p a pint (or less) it is possible that crafted ales and beers will be a natural response to economic crises. The miners did it, and on the 25th anniversary of their struggles maybe we will need to learn from them again:

> Like many other workers we were all pretty good in our different ways at making ends meet. John had always been ace at making home brew, and as the years went by he became really excellent at producing exquisite tastes from virtually anything. He even said he could make a fine wine out of rank, sweaty socks and reckoned we'd all enjoy it! Certainly he knew what flowers and weeds to pick from the countryside for those special flavours. One of his specialities was tea wine and during the strike the tea leaf strainer was in constant use everywhere as he became the village tester (and taster) in chief, always taking along his thermometer and gauges to test the myriad fermenting brews of wine and beer.
>
> *The Miners: Jenny Tells Her Tale* from Revoltagainstplenty.com

Chris Carlsson in his recent book *Nowtopia* documents the myriad of non-wage labour 'work' that people are engaging in, both as an exodus from the social factory (the invasion of capitalism into everything and everywhere) and the means of building communities strong enough to challenge the system of commodity production. So home brewing is back! Gleaning returns! Could there be a resurgence of the ale-stake or strange red and green tactics of wildcrafting for wildcats?

> I'm not comfortable with home brewing. It seems fraught with mischief to me. Maybe I don't understand it.

Gregory Bell, one of three politicians to vote against the recent legalisation home brewing in Utah, USA, Feb 2009.

Part 2 - Nettle Beer : Or How To Brew a Different Social Relationship Based on Commoning Rather Than Alienation

(including a brief exploration of 800 years of history including both the use of Structural Adjustment Policies by the IMF and of the use of sugar in making alcohol)

Recipe

For your pleasure here is the recipe for 'King Gone!' a pre-enclosure herb flavoured ale brewed for BRHG's *Off With Their Heads!* event in November 2008. It is a 'plaque-ale', created to raise money for public works like the Seven Stars Plaque.

> 1 kg malt extract
> 1 kg of brown sugar
> 1 spoon of yeast
> 1 oz of yarrow, nettles and 20 juniper berries
> Makes 5 gallons (40 pints)

Mix the malt extract with 1 gallon of hot water, and stir in the sugar until dissolved. Meanwhile in 2 gallons of hot water boil the herbs (yarrow, nettle and juniper berries) for an hour. Strain the herb water into a big bucket and mix in the malt. Add 2 gallons of cold water to make it lukewarm for the yeast. For a stronger brew add a sachet of brewers' yeast, otherwise activate a spoon of bread yeast in 200ml of warm water with a spoon of sugar, when it is frothy add to the ale. Cover the bucket, and leave in a warm place. After 10 days it is probably ready to siphon into a 5 gallon brewing barrel (or you can use plastic pop bottles.) Leave for 2 weeks and it should be ready!

The Philosophy of Collecting Nettles

Until recently I had no experience of brewing beer, but I did have an interesting revelation/discovery courtesy of Peter Linebaugh, the US-based radical historian. The revelation occurred during an event organised by Bristol Radical History Group called *Down with the Fences: Struggle for the Global Commons*. It concerned a hidden history of the rights of commoners to subsistence and existence from public and private land. These rights were catalogued in a document called *The Charter of Forest* written down in 1215. This document in essence enshrined in law the notion of the commons, and its 'brother' document the Magna Carta, referred to the legal and political rights (trial by jury, the right to remain silent) that we have taken for granted even as they are under attack today. The two documents together defined limits to **privatisation** (a word relation to **deprivation**).[1]

To collect nettles from public or private land is a process of **usufruct** (temporary possession, or use of the advantages of another persons property). It is making use of **waste** (in legal terms - a piece of land not in any individuals occupation, lying in common). So to take nettles and then transform them into a brew for intoxication at a **folkmote** (deliberate gathering of people, a general assembly, soviet or meeting) could be seen as a act of **commoning**.[2]

By **commoning** you are moving away from the quaint practises of a yonder imagining tomorrow. It is a verb describing any activity or process designed increase the availability of the commons in everyday life. That is, the notion something held in common, something that is free, outside of money exchar (but not a free for all). It is the protection of public resources from privatisati and enclosure, not by conservation and well meaning that are nevertheless para enclosures, but a protection through an economic and direct relationship t resists the museumification of nature. The Diggers, the 16th Century Agrar

Communists, who occupied St Georges Hill in Surrey to resist the removal of both themselves and their livelihoods from the landscape, knew this and planted corn to confirm it.

With all this in mind I set out to practice a bit of **herbiage** (the right to collect herbs), in this case an attempt to make five gallons (forty pints) of nettle brew.

I collected the nettles, (two hundred **lops and tops**. I can now call them lops and tops, invoking the right to take cuttings or trimmings from foliage superfluous growth), from Royate Hill Community Allotment in Bristol.

one minded as there were quite a lot and I regulate my use. If I tried to take ·m all I'm sure someone would have come over and disputed what I was doing.

·er gathering the nettles I went home, gave them a rinse, put them in a large pot, led three gallons of water and brought to the boil. Watching the gas flicker on stove made me think of **firebote** (the right to gather firewood for fuel) and I 1embered hearing about a proposed 'Hydrocarbon Commons' called for by the :atistas of Mexico and the Ijaw in Nigeria[3]. These proposals made me think ·ut the economist Garret Hardin who in the 1960s wrote a text called Tragedy of the Commons. It talked of ecologies being destroyed and degraded because they are held in common. Because they are not a commodity - that is they have no (exchange) value - so in order for them to be protected and regulated they should be privatised. This way people will value them and be sensible in their use. He ignored thousands of years of communal negotiation and custom. He removed from the commons the very people that sustained the land, and in doing so provided the pretext for IMF/World Bank Structural Adjustment Policies. Ironically, the forces he contended would protect the land - the free market - were the very ones that accelerated the degradation of the land to the point where we are now at the point of eco-systemic failure.

Our notion that self management is possible, and of the possibilities of autonomy, seem far far away in the UK. After the class struggles of the 70s, and the consequent flight of capital to lands far away, the intensification of work and the commodification of everything including culture - especially culture - gives the impression of a movement seemingly in retreat.

The brew was served up to thirsty punters during the Sunday night cafe at Kebele, a radical social centre in Bristol:

Kebele is a space for organising, supporting and campaigning autonomously. Kebele is a community co-operative, run by volunteers on a not-for-profit basis and providing an alternative social space. We organise collectively without leaders and oppose all forms of authority. A co-operative is an autonomous association of persons united voluntarily to meet their common economic, social and cultural needs and aspirations through a jointly-owned and democratically controlled enterprise.[4]

The brew in total cost £6, funded with donations and £1 commission from The Eccentric City.

For other recipes and artworks concerning the commons see http://www.stuffit.org

Steve Stuffit 2008[5]

Further Reading / References

Revolt Against Plenty website: http://www.revoltagainstplenty.com
Alcohol, No Ordinary Commodity by Linda Hill
Class Conflict and the Crisis of Feudalism by Rodney Howard Hilton
History of English Ale and Beer by H. A. Monckton
Beer and Britannia: An Inebriated History of Britain by Peter Haydon
A History of Beer and Brewing by Ian Spencer Hornsey
Plenty and Want by John Burnett
The Agrarian History of England and Wales by E. J. T. Collins
The Brewing Industry in England 1700-1830 by Peter Mathias
The village Ale-Wife: Women and Brewing in Fourteenth Century England by Judith Bennett
Witchcraft in early modern Europe by By Jonathan Barry, Marianne Hester, Gareth Roberts
Sacred and Herbal Healing Beers: The Secrets of Ancient Fermentation by Stephen Harrod Buhner

1. See Peter Linebaughs book *The Magna Carta Manifesto: Commons and Liberties for All*
2. See Massimo De Angelis book *The Beginning of History: Value Stuggles & Global Capital*: http://www.commoner.org.uk/
3. See George Caffentzis *The Petroleum Commons*: http://www.counterpunch.org/caffentzis12152004.html
4. See Kebele Social Centre Website http://www.kebelecoop.org/
5. A 'Steve' is a piece of working class east london slang that referred to going back to someone's house after the pub I.e. 'Would you like to go for a steve?

This is a journey from pre-enclosure herbal brews made by ale-wives to the domination of hops and large breweries. But don't despair, this is a return trip thanks to the rediscovery of commoning and a recipe for nettle and juniper ale.

ISBN 978-1-911522-11-9